Solid Foundation

LIFE OF PETER

*Blueprints for 30 messages
built upon God's Word*

F. Sherwood Smith

Cincinnati, Ohio

Cover design by Grannan Graphic Design LTD

Interior design by Robert E. Korth

Edited by Jim Eichenberger
© 2000 by Standard Publishing
All rights reserved.
Printed in the U.S.A.

Solid Foundation™ is a trademark of
Standard Publishing, Cincinnati, Ohio.
A division of Standex International Corporation.
07 06 05 04 03 02 01 00   5 4 3 2 1

Contents

Peter's Heritage

Various Passages

Peter was a man of humble beginnings. A Galilean by birth, he was a resident of Bethsaida, which means "house of fish" (John 1:44). This insignificant village was located north of Capernaum, near Chorazin, possibly on the western shore of the Sea of Galilee. Not to be confused with Bethsaida-Julias, a much more populous and important city located at the northeast end of the sea near to where Jesus fed the 5000, Peter's hometown was a sleepy little burg of no obvious consequence. Yet in this village, God shaped the early years of this great apostle.

I.   PETER EXHIBITED AN INTEREST IN SEEKING GOD'S WORD.

A. Peter was willing to venture outside of the comfort zone of his hometown to seek God's messenger.

1. When Peter is introduced in the gospel story, he is brought to our attention as being in Judea, near to the capital city, Jerusalem.
2. Peter's purpose for being in Judea was that he was a disciple of John the Baptist.

B. Peter left his job as partner in a fishing venture (Luke 5:10) to be a student under the teaching of John the Baptist.

1. John's ministry was located southeast of Jerusalem at the river Jordan where he baptized penitent believers.
2. One can stand on the remains of ancient Jericho and look six miles to the east where a green ribbon of vegetation is plainly visible along Jordan's banks. West from Jericho to Jerusalem was eighteen miles.
3. When the Pharisees and Sadducees (Matthew 3:7) and the people of Jerusalem (Mark 1:5) went to where John was baptizing, they traveled about twenty-four miles.
4. This is the area where Peter, his brother Andrew, and friends had come to study under the instruction of John.

II.   THIS INTEREST CAME FROM HIS HOME AND FAMILY.

A. Peter was given a significant name at birth.

1. His parents gave him the meaningful Hebrew name of Simeon (cf. Acts 15:14). Both the Hebrew and Greek forms of the name stem from root words meaning "to hear." We could easily imagine Peter, like "The

Drummer Boy" in the Christmas song, in awe and wonder asking his companions as they listened to Jesus, "Do you hear what I hear?"
2. If his parents were still alive, one wonders what they thought when Jesus called their son "Peter, the rock."

B. In youth Peter would have received typical Jewish teaching and training grounded in Scriptures and schooled in the synagogue.
1. Jewish parents were directed in the law to constantly review the commandments of the Lord with their children (Deuteronomy 6:4-9; 11:18-21).
2. Jewish boys living with their parents in Galilee traveled to the Passover and other feasts. Much of their religious history was involved in instructional symbolism in the feasts.

C. The influence of home and parental training continues to be forceful and formative today.
1. Having passed my seventy-sixth birthday I can still see vividly the 10 x 12 size pictures Mother held on her knees and hear her voice reading the Bible stories of Daniel, David and Goliath, and the Hebrew children in the fiery furnace. They laid the foundation of faith in God in a little boy's heart. Mother could not have imagined in those moments of sharing with her son that he would mature to be a Bible college professor for more than three decades.
2. Shirley Wallingford placed notes of Scripture in her sons' school lunches, pinned them on basketball uniforms when she finished laundering them, attached them to the pillowcases on which they slept. Their basketball coach and his family were led to the Lord. Today, Tim preaches the gospel in Louisville, KY, and Tony is the basketball coach at a Christian college.

CONCLUSION

Consider the kind of training Peter and his brother must have received to influence them to be far from home in search of knowledge concerning the coming Messiah.

Are parents afraid to pray the prayer of Luke 10:2 for fear their children may answer their prayer?

Peter's Spiritual Mentor

Matthew 3:1-12; Mark 1:1-8;
Luke 3:1-20; John 1:19-28

The mission of John the Baptist was to "prepare the way for the Lord." One of the ways John fulfilled his mission was to prepare disciples like Peter to become apostles of Jesus. John prepared Peter by declaring clearly who he was and why he had come.

I. **JOHN WAS THE FORERUNNER OF THE MESSIAH (LUKE 3:4-6; MARK 1:1-3).**
   A. John played a unique role in God's plan.
      1. His position was unique. John was the intermediary between the Old Testament Levitical sacrificial system and the New Covenant which would be initiated by Jesus.
      2. His methods were unique. John preached repentance and baptism as the new way to find forgiveness of sin and acceptance with God (Matthew 3:1-6; Mark 1:4). Though the claim has been made that Jews practiced proselyte baptism long before the time of Christ, both Jewish and Christian scholars have found no conclusive evidence of such a claim. John was a very common name. If baptisms were common and Jews had been performing them for decades, how would the designation "Baptist" distinguish this particular John?
      3. His message was unique. The Jewish leaders knew that John's teaching was completely innovative and would cancel the law's requirements.
      4. His authority was unique. On Monday of the last week of Jesus' life, his struggle with Jewish authorities was intense. They wanted to know by what authority Jesus operated. Jesus claimed that his personal authority and that of John the Baptist were identical (Matthew 21:23-27).

   B. The person and role of John was predicted.
      1. The last Old Testament prophecy speaks of him (Malachi 4:5, 6).
      2. His role was described to his father before he was conceived (Luke 1:14-17).

II. **JOHN CONFESSED THAT HE WAS NOT THE CHRIST (MARK 1:7, 8; LUKE 3:15-17).**
   A. Jesus would have greater authority and works. "After me will come one more powerful than I" (Mark 1:7).

7

B. Jesus would have a higher position. John described the Messiah as one "the thongs of whose sandals I am not worthy to stoop down and untie" (Mark 1:7).

C. Jesus would have produced more complete results. "I baptize you with water, but he will baptize you with the Holy Spirit" (Mark 1:8).

D. Jesus would handle sin fully. Jesus will "gather the wheat into his barn, but he will burn up the chaff with unquenchable fire" (Luke 3:17).

III. JOHN CONFESSED THAT HE WAS NOT THE PROPHET ELIJAH (JOHN 1:21).

A. Reincarnation is not taught in the Bible, but is common in paganism.
  1. Life after death is taught from Genesis to Revelation.
  2. It is appointed to man once to die (Hebrews 9:27).

B. It was predicted that John would possess "the spirit and power of Elijah" (Luke 1:17).
  1. The "spirit . . . of Elijah" has reference to his mind-set and commitment.
  2. John performed no miracles as did Elijah, but he possessed tremendous revelatory powers.
  3. He was more than a prophet (Matthew 11:9). None other than Moses had ever bridged dispensations of God as did John. There was no one born of woman who was greater than John (Luke 7:28).

CONCLUSION

What a privilege for Peter to sit at the feet of a teacher like John! He was taught of the Messiah he would later serve. He also was taught the humility necessary to serve the Savior without usurping his authority.

ILLUSTRATION

Holy Spirit and fire. In a Pentecostal church service where all prayed vocally at once, a gentleman standing close to me prayed for God to send the Holy Spirit and the fire. Obviously he thought "fire" represented some blessing and did not associate it with judgment. I knew I had already received the Holy Spirit when I was baptized and I prayed silently that God would save me from the fire of his judgment (Malachi 4:1, 2).

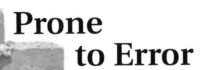

Prone to Error

Matthew 16:21-23; 26:69-75; Galatians 2:11-16

If we learn from our mistakes, Peter had plenty of opportunities to gain wisdom! Yet those who never make a mistake never accomplish anything. Peter seemed to live by the philosophy, "It is better to do some things wrong than to do nothing at all." Let us examine three general errors to which Peter was prone.

I. **PETER ATTEMPTED TO DISSUADE JESUS FROM GOING TO THE CROSS (MATTHEW 16:21-23).**
   A. Peter had just made the grand, good confession (vv. 13-20).
      1. He had just received the meaningful, spiritual, and symbolic name of Peter.
      2. He had just been promised the "keys of the kingdom."

   B. Immediately thereafter he was ready to argue with Jesus.
      1. He rebuked the Lord (v. 22).
      2. He blatantly affirmed that what Jesus said would happen could never occur.

   C. Jesus told Peter he was being used as a tool of the devil. This earthly mindset contrasted with Jesus' heavenly mission. Moments after being called "the rock," this same rock was becoming a stumbling block to Jesus (v. 23).

   D. Peter was still making the same error in the Garden of Gethsemane, trying to prevent Jesus' arrest with swordplay (John 18:10).
      1. Many think the sword in this instance was actually a very large knife used in the preparation of the Passover lamb.
      2. If Peter's actions were proper, "How then would the Scriptures be fulfilled?" (Matthew 26:54).
      3. More than seventy-two thousand angels were available if such action as that of Peter was within God's will (Matthew 26:53).

II. **PETER ALLOWED HIS PREJUDICE TO HINDER CHRISTIAN FELLOWSHIP WITH GENTILES AT ANTIOCH (GALATIANS 2:11-16).**
   A. This occurred even after Peter had received special divine instruction at

9

Joppa and the unique experience at Caesarea which followed (Acts 10, 11).

B. Peter also played a significant role in the conference on circumcision held at Jerusalem (Acts 15:7-11).
1. He referred to his experience at Caesarea (vv. 7, 14).
2. He cited the prophets as authority on the subject (vv. 15-18).
3. He concluded that both Jew and Gentile were saved by "the grace of our Lord Jesus." (This is the first time the word "grace" is used by Peter.)

C. Peter had proper knowledge, but in weakness he feared the Jerusalem Jews more than he feared truth and God (Galatians 2:12).

D. There are those who seek to defend Peter by suggesting that if Paul had the right to avoid affront or harm to others by avoiding certain foods or drink, then Peter should have the privilege of avoiding that which was a problem to his Jewish brethren. Paul's judgment was that Peter was in error (Galatians 2:11).

III.   PETER ALLOWED FEAR TO DISTANCE HIM FROM JESUS (MATTHEW 26:69-75).

A. Significantly, all four Gospels record Peter's denials of Jesus. (See also Mark 14:66-72; Luke 22:54-62; and John 18:25-27.) The records vary greatly but there is no contradiction. Many persons, both men and women, were questioning Peter's association with Jesus. The fact that John quotes a male servant and the synoptics quote a female servant should create no alarm. Also, John's statement (like Matthew's and Luke's), "the cock crew" is a general statement, while Mark's account, "before the cock crow twice," is a specific statement.

B. We may speculate upon the motivation for the denials.
1. His denials may have been motivated by fear. Nevertheless, there is a vast difference between fear and cowardice. Peter was no coward. His defense of Jesus and his leadership in the church prove his courageous character. Even the most courageous may give in to fear on occasion.
2. His denials may have been simply motivated by the universal and normal function of self-preservation.
3. Peter knew that he had failed and he "wept bitterly."

ILLUSTRATION

Fear vs. cowardice. An influential preacher on the West Coast served in the Navy in his early years. On one tour, in rough seas, his friend whom he knew could not swim well fell overboard. He could swim well but the huge waves and the forceful undertow of the great propellers which drove the ship filled his mind with fear. He was afraid, but no coward. He dived in and saved the life of his friend.

A Complex Personality

Various Passages

It is easy to point to weaknesses and errors by Peter. Yet his personality is intriguing and attractive. He is described as the "most human" of all the apostles and as being "simple and natural." Obviously he was a very complex person possessing a multifaceted make-up.

I. PETER POSSESSED AN ACTIVE MIND.

   A. Peter answered two critical questions when others failed to do so.

     1. Jesus asked, "You do not want to leave too, do you?" (John 6:67). Peter's insightful answer was, "Lord, to whom shall we go? You have the words of eternal life" (v. 68).

     2. Jesus asked, "Who do you say I am?" The good confession came from the lips of Peter (Matthew 16:15, 16).

   B. Peter was quick to ask questions.

     1. Many times people refuse to ask questions for fear they will appear foolish. It was a great learning experience for Peter.

     2. Jesus had been teaching about forgiveness (Matthew 18:15-17). Peter's inquiring mind posed the question: "How many times shall I forgive?" (Matthew 18:21).

     3. When Jesus was ready to close his ministry on earth, he said, "Where I am going you cannot come" (John 13:33). Peter had heard Jesus say repeatedly, "Follow me." Immediately Peter wanted to know, "Where are you going? Why can't I follow you?" (John 13:36, 37). After the resurrection Peter understood "follow me!" (John 21:19).

   C. Peter placed great emphasis upon knowledge.

     1. In the opening of the second epistle (2 Peter 1:2-8), Peter refers to knowledge five times. He not only used the most common word for knowledge *(gnosis)*, but began and ended with the compound form *(epignosis)* which intensified the meaning. It is knowledge upon knowledge; full knowledge.

     2. His last written instruction is "grow in . . . knowledge" (2 Peter 3:18).

   D. Peter was open to correction.

     1. In the upper room, when Jesus wanted to wash his feet, Peter objected,

"You shall never wash my feet" (John 13:8). When the lesson was understood Peter said, "Not just my feet but my hands and my head" (head to foot) (John 13:9).

2. When being prepared to preach to Gentiles, Peter again objected, "I have never eaten anything . . . unclean," (Acts 10:14). But Peter later understood the spiritual significance of God's directives and made the correction (Acts 10:34, 35).

II. PETER POSSESSED A NOBLE CHARACTER.

A. Peter had high ideals.

1. He urged his readers to pursue a virtuous life of self-control, patience, godliness, and brotherly kindness (2 Peter 1:5-7), and to put away all deceit, hypocrisy, envy, and slander (1 Peter 2:1).
2. Peter not only lived his ideals, he was willing to die for them (Matthew 26:35).

B. Peter was independent and exercised personal initiative.

1. Jesus said to Peter, "When you were younger you . . . went where you wanted" (John 21:18). He had a mind of his own.
2. At the time of Jesus' arrest, Peter cut off the ear of the servant of the high priest, in a rash attempt to protect Jesus (John 18:10).
3. Peter was the first to approach the empty tomb (Luke 24:12).
4. When the Sanhedrin imposed a "gag order" on his preaching, Peter refused to comply, saying, "We must obey God rather than men!" (Acts 5:29).

C. Peter was decisive.

1. In dealing with Ananias and Sapphira (Acts 5:1-11), Peter recognized that immediate and decisive action was essential to maintain integrity in the infant church.
2. God backed Peter by exacting severe punishment.

D. Peter possessed a tender compassionate heart.

1. One can hear the growing emphasis with which he spoke when he shared last moments with Jesus. Three times he affirmed, "You know that I love you" (John 21:15-17).
2. Though often misguided, Peter's heart was devoted to Jesus. In the upper room he promised, "I will lay down my life for you" (John 13:37). History tells us that eventually that promise was kept.

Unforgettable Steps

Matthew 14; John 6

Peter surely reminisced at length about deeply meaningful experiences shared with Jesus. During the thirty-seven years between the death of Jesus and his own, stories must have poured from his lips like water from an artesian well. One of those stories actually occurred on water. No doubt it was stamped on his mind like words engraved in marble.

I. THE SETTING

A. The disciples were experiencing a wide range of conflicting emotions.
   1. John the Baptist was beheaded. His disciples buried him and came to tell Jesus (Matthew 14:1-12). Where else could they go?
   2. Jesus withdrew privately with his disciples, providing a time for comfort and encouragement. At least half of the apostles had been disciples of John (Matthew 14:13).
   3. Crowds followed Jesus as he fed five thousand (Matthew 14:13-21). This tremendous "high" came on the heels of the tremendous "low" of John's death.

B. The apostles were beginning to balk at Jesus' leadership (Matthew 14:22, 23).
   1. Jewish revolutionaries (Zealots) threatened to take Jesus by force and make him king (John 6:15). For the disciples this was a "high," but for Jesus great disappointment.
   2. Jesus ordered his disciples to cross the sea to remove them from such worldly influence. They could not rise above the earthly concept, even after the resurrection (Acts 1:6).
   3. The disciples did not obey the directions of Jesus to go to the other side of the sea (Matthew 14:22; John 6:16).

C. Jesus went alone into the mountain to pray (Matthew 14:23).
   1. He must have left during the first watch (6-9 P.M.), because he was in the mountain "when evening came." It was during the fourth watch (3-6 A.M.), that Jesus came down to the sea (Matthew 14:25).
   2. By morning the apostles should have rowed the six miles across to Capernaum. Instead they were in the middle of the sea (John 6:19).

II.   THE MIRACLE
    A. Jesus approached the boat.
        1. The disciples thought they saw a ghost. They were terrified and cried out in fear (Matthew 14:26; John 6:19).
        2. Jesus identified himself and calmed their fears (Matthew 14:27; John 6:20).

    B. Peter wanted to approach Jesus (Matthew 14:28-33).
        1. "Lord, if it's you, . . . tell me to come to you on the water" (v. 28).
        2. Peter began his walk, but when he saw the results of the wind, his fear subverted his efforts (v. 29; John 6:18).

III.   THE LESSONS (JOHN 6:16-21)
    A. The accounts of the Gospels are factual and should never be reduced to myth in order to teach figurative lessons.
        1. Matthew and John wrote as eyewitnesses.
        2. Notice the strong evidential content of John 6:22-25.

    B. There are some practical figurative applications which can be extracted from John's account and applied to the church.
        1. "It was dark"; picture the dark world and Christians in the old "Ship of Zion" pulling at the oars in the face of great odds.
        2. "Jesus had not yet joined them." We anticipate his promised return (John 14:3).
        3. He was seen "approaching." (See Revelation 22:20 and Romans 13:11.)
        4. The disciples were "willing to take him into the boat." What a rapturous moment when he comes for his church-bride.
        5. "Immediately" they were at their destination. Does John mean to introduce another miraculous element? They were in the middle of the sea, but immediately at shore. In a moment, we will be changed and at our eternal home (1 Corinthians 15:51, 52).

ILLUSTRATION
What Jesus calls us to do. In a chapel sermon, Dr. Lewis Foster once reminded his seminarians that Jesus did not command Peter to walk on water. His invitation was, "Come to me."

Restoration of Peter

John 21:15-23

After the resurrection, the memory of his denial of Christ surely still haunted Peter. Mired in uncertainty and guilt, Peter returned to what he knew best—the fishing business. Yet in the midst of his funk, he could not even do this right! After fishing all night with some fellow disciples, he caught nothing.

A distant figure called from the shore at dawn. When the disciples cast their net on the other side of the boat as the stranger instructed, the net was filled with fish. Recognizing this miracle as the one performed when Jesus had first called him (Luke 5:3-7), Peter recognized both the messenger and his message. He was ready to renew his relationship with the master whom he had abandoned.

I.   JESUS HAD PETER REAFFIRM HIS LOVE FOR HIM.
   A. "Simon son of John, do you truly love me more than these?" (v. 15).
   1. To a once-proud disciple who seemed to enjoy being in the forefront, Jesus may have been asking, "Do you love me more than your fellow-disciples love me?"
   2. To a discouraged disciple who may have been considering going back to his old occupation, Jesus may have been asking, "Do you love me more than this fishing business?"
   3. Peter did not address the qualifier, but simply affirmed his love for Jesus.

   B. Much is made of the choice of words made by Jesus and by Peter. Both words translated "love" are very meaningful.
   1. Jesus used *agapao* the first two times he questioned Peter's love. This word is usually said to express a God-like love which demands nothing in return.
   2. Jesus used *phileo* in the third question. This word is sometimes translated "affection" but also frequently "love." ("Philadelphia" means "city of brotherly love.")
   3. Peter answered with *phileo* all three times.

II.   JESUS REMINDED PETER OF THE COST OF DISCIPLESHIP.
   A. Three times Peter was commanded to care for the charges of the Good Shepherd.
   1. "Feed my lambs" (v. 15). The word *arnion* used here means a "little lamb."
   2. "Take care of my sheep" (v. 16). The verb used here is derived from the

noun meaning "shepherd." The object of the verb is *probaton*, meaning sheep.

3. "Feed my sheep" (v. 17). A third word is used as the object here, *probation*, meaning "dear little sheep."

B. Jesus predicted that Peter would die a martyr's death (vv. 18, 19).

C. Peter was told to follow Jesus regardless of what happened to other believers (vv. 20-23).

1. Jesus reaffirmed his sovereignty over the lives of both Peter and John with the reply, "If I want him to remain alive until I return, what is that to you?"

2. John notes that this remark was twisted to begin a rumor that Jesus promised that John would not die. Even after John's death the legend grew. Stories were told about the ground rising and falling over the grave of John at Ephesus as he continued to breathe after burial.

ILLUSTRATION

The three-fold challenge. Roman tradition has it that their legionaries were challenged three times before going into battle. The third question was, "Are you ready to die for Caesar?" The soldiers would then raise their spears and shields high in the air and vociferously shout in the affirmative, "We are ready to die for Caesar."

Peter's martyrdom. The *Domine Quo Vadis* tradition gained popularity in the fourth century. It held that Peter was leaving Rome because of the severe persecution under Nero's reign. Peter was slinking out of the city on the Appian Way and met the Lord going the opposite direction. Peter said to Jesus, *Domine Quo Vadis* ("Lord, where are you going?") Jesus responded, "I am going into the city to suffer with my people." Peter said, "I am going with you, Lord." He returned to Rome where he was crucified with his head to the ground because he said, "I am not worthy to die as did my Lord."

The First Gospel Preacher

Acts 2

Preachers struggle for sensational sermon "starters." They have been trained to do so to center attention and establish rapport with their audience. Though Peter had no teaching in homiletics or public speaking, he received help from Heaven in introducing a crucial sermon.

Before he spoke his audience was greeted with the sound of a tornado, but no movement of air. They witnessed flames of fire but no heat or smoke. As evidence of the empowering presence of the Holy Spirit, Peter and all the other apostles were enabled to speak in languages not native to them. Therefore, those in Jerusalem on that day of Pentecost were divinely prepared to hear the first gospel sermon.

I. PETER UNDERSTOOD HIS DIFFICULT AUDIENCE.

A. They were homogeneous in faith.

1. The vast majority of his hearers were Jewish by faith.
2. Peter addressed, "Fellow Jews and all of you who live in Jerusalem" (v. 14).

B. They were heterogeneous in nationality and culture.

1. At Passover well over one million Jews came from all over the known world to celebrate. Many who traveled great distances remained in Jerusalem the fifty days between Passover and Pentecost. Although they were all Jews, language, clothing, and everyday customs varied greatly.
2. Large numbers of those who came to the feasts were converts to the Jewish faith. Though Jewish, they were not descendants of Abraham.

II. PETER CLEARLY STATED THE FACTS CONCERNING JESUS.

A. Supernatural phenomena ("miracles, wonders and signs") authenticated Jesus' ministry (v. 22).

1. "Miracles" were demonstrations of great power.
2. These miracles served as "signs," presenting evidence that pointed to Jesus' divine authority.
3. These miracles resulted in "wonder," inspiring awe and reverence toward Jesus.

B. The crucifixion was fallen humankind's reaction to meeting God face-to-face (v. 23).

17

1. God knew beforehand, but foreknowledge should never be equated with cause. The cause was humankind's wickedness.
2. It was in God's plan for Jesus to give his life, but he was not "programmed" for death. Jesus' struggle in Gethsemane clearly illustrates that he had freedom of choice in his sacrificial death.

C. By the resurrection, death was conquered (vv. 24-32).
1. The resurrection of Jesus is attributed to all three members of the Godhead (Romans 8:11; John 10:17, 18).
2. Peter's emphasis is upon God's action (vv. 24, 32).

D. With his ascension, Jesus assumed Lordship over creation (vv. 33-35).
1. Jesus was exalted to the right hand of God.
2. In this position, Jesus serves as the intercessor between God and humanity (Hebrews 7:25).
3. We are "saved through his life" (Romans 5:10).

III. PETER LED THE CROWD TO A LOGICAL CONCLUSION
A. God made Jesus to be both Lord and Christ (v. 36).
1. He is the Christ, the Messiah of Israel, the appointed and anointed one.
2. He is our Lord, the authority for our faith and actions.
3. Jesus, his personal name ("Christ" being his title), has the root meaning of "salvation."

B. Jesus' work demands a personal response (v. 37).
1. We must repent and be baptized, accepting God's forgiveness of sins and the indwelling of the promised Holy Spirit (v. 38).
2. This was not just to be the response of the original hearers of this sermon. The same response is required to this day (v. 39).

ILLUSTRATION
Cultural differences. After traveling around the world more than once, I've been forced to admit that a universal "Christian dress code" does not exist. In one country, that which is wholly acceptable is very improper in the very next country visited. That which is considered to be decent and proper varies greatly among committed Christians even in the various areas and cultures of America. Surely it was so in the whole world known to Peter, not only with respect to clothing but in a multitude of other practices as well. We are not united by superficial marks, but rather by the unifying work of Christ.

The First to Introduce the Last

Acts 2:16, 17

With the arrival of a new millennium, many speak with fervor concerning the "last days." Centuries ago, Peter first addressed the church on that topic. Peter was greatly privileged to be not only the first gospel preacher, but also to be the first to discuss God's closing transactions with his people.

I. THE TRADITIONAL VIEWS OF "LAST DAYS"

A. The evangelical world in general promotes the concept of "last days" as being some rather limited, parenthetical period of time at the close of human history.

1. Frequently so-called proof passages are cited such as 1 Timothy 4:1-3. All of the negative characteristics of this text are present today so they conclude we are in the "later times" and thus the coming of Christ is imminent.

2. The truth is, however, that those same characteristics were present in Paul's day and in every succeeding generation to the present.

B. One's expectations of the "last days" are often driven by his or her interpretation of the thousand year period (millennium) described in Revelation 20:1-6.

1. Pre-millennialists believe that Jesus will return to a troubled, apostate world, put things right, and then rule on earth for one thousand years. Therefore, *increased rejection* of the gospel is seen as a sign of the last days.

2. Post-millennialists believe that the church will eventually evangelize the world, leading to an unprecedented millennial period of peace in which Christ rules through the church. Therefore, *increased interest* in the gospel is seen as a sign of the last days.

II. PETER'S VIEW OF THE LAST DAYS

A. Peter refers to the prophet Joel's statement about the last days (Joel 2:28-32).

1. Peter's statement came in response to the amazement and perplexity caused when the apostles spoke in languages they had never learned (Acts 2:12).

2. Peter indicated that this miracle was the fulfillment of Joel's prophecy, indicating that the last days had begun on that day of Pentecost (2:16).

B. Peter probably understood the "last days" to be the time during which the Son of God would grant eternal life to all who believe (John 5:24-27).

1. This is that period of time known as the gospel age or the Christian dispensation or the Messianic era.
2. This is a time in which people will hear the message of Jesus and be converted from death in sin to life in Christ.
3. An ethical resurrection occurs. Life is lived on an entirely different, elevated plane (2 Corinthians 5:17; Ephesians 2:1-6).

C. Writings of other apostles labeled the times in which they lived as the "last days."
1. "Dear children, this is the last hour" (1 John 2:18). The appearance of many teachers whose doctrines were "antichrist" was evidence to John that it was the "last hour." John's reasoning seems to be that antichrists could only come if the true Christ had already come. Furthermore, if the Christ has come, it must be the last hour because God's final message to man had been spoken.
2. "He was chosen before the creation of the world, but was revealed in these last times for your sake" (1 Peter 1:20). Peter also argues that the "last times" are the days in which the gospel of Christ is proclaimed.
3. "In the past God spoke to our forefathers through the prophets at many times and in various ways, but in these last days he has spoken to us by his Son" (Hebrews 1:1, 2).
4. "But now he [Christ] has appeared once for all at the end of the ages to do away with sin by the sacrifice of himself" (Hebrews 9:26). Clearly the "the end of the ages" has reference to the entire Christian dispensation from the birth of the church on Pentecost to the second coming of Christ and judgment.

CONCLUSION

We think of the last days as the time immediately preceding the second coming of Christ. Peter and the other apostles had a much broader definition. They knew that they were in the "last days," a period beginning at the birth of the church and concluding with the second coming. In Jesus, God began to bring salvation history to a conclusion. There will never be another Savior, another sacrifice for sin, or another covenant between God and man. We are in the last days of God's plan for humanity.

ILLUSTRATIONS

Accepting God's plan for the end. A respected college professor claimed to be a "pro-millennialist." He was in total agreement and acquiescence to whatever God intended to do in reference to a millennium. Another said he was a "pan-millennialist." However it all pans out was all right with him.

Divisiveness of millennial views. A student said he was so opposed to post-millennial view and so committed to pre-millennialism that he couldn't even eat Post Toasties®.

The First Apostolic Healing Miracle

Acts 3

The first miracle performed by the apostles was speaking in languages which were unfamiliar to them (Acts 2:4). After that account, Luke states, "Many wonders and miraculous signs were done by the apostles" (2:43). With these words he introduces a sampling of the mighty acts of God which demonstrated the authority given to the first ambassadors of the New Covenant. The first healing miracle he records is found in chapter three of Acts.

I.   THE OCCASION
A. Peter and John went to the temple to pray at 3:00 P.M.
   1. They approached Solomon's Colonnade (3:11) and the gate of the temple designated "Beautiful" (3:2).
   2. A man lame from birth was placed at the gate daily to beg. He asked alms of Peter and John.

B. The apostles did have economic potential.
   1. When Jesus was with the apostles they had a treasury (John 13:27-30). Food and other essentials were purchased for their use. Funds from this treasury were also shared with the poor.
   2. On this occasion Peter indicated that he had no coin to give, but he could bestow blessing as a result of the miraculous power which was vested in him.

II.   THE MIRACLE
A. Healing came from the power of Jesus within the apostles, not from the apostles themselves. "In the name of Jesus Christ of Nazareth, walk" (3:6).
   1. This was an exercise of power promised to apostles. Luke 24:49 records the promise that they would be "clothed with power from on high."
   2. The apostles had been chosen by Jesus, appointed and empowered by him (John 15:16). They were a unique band. They had been promised that they would perform miracles as Jesus himself had (John 14:11-14).

B. Physical action accompanied the miracle, but did nothing to cause it. "Taking him by the right hand, he [Peter] helped him up" (v. 7).
   1. Frequently in connection with biblical miracles some action was taken to help the one in need to increase in faith. Jesus commanded the

invalid by the Pool of Bethesda to take up his mat and walk (John 5:8). In healing a man born blind, Jesus put mud on the man's eyes and ordered him to wash in the Pool of Siloam (John 9:6).

2. No more power was in the hand of Peter than in the mud or the mat (Acts 3:12). The power was resident in the name of Jesus alone.

III. THE RESULTS

A. The man was healed physically and renewed spiritually (vv. 7-11).

1. "He jumped to his feet and began to walk."
2. "He went with them into the temple courts, walking and jumping, and praising God."
3. He "held on to Peter and John."

B. The crowd's amazement and wonder created a teachable moment (v. 10).

1. Peter first turned attention from himself to Jesus (vv. 11-16). This pattern is repeated in apostolic preaching. Peter would later refuse to be worshiped by Cornelius (Acts 10:25, 26). Paul and Barnabas were appalled when the people of Lystra wanted to offer sacrifices to them (Acts 14:8-18).
2. The miracle created a great opportunity to call the listeners to faith in Jesus (vv. 17-26).

CONCLUSION

God's providential care is still exerted, and prayers are still being answered. From this first recorded apostolic healing miracle to this day, God still works through his servants to make men and women whole. We must note that the purpose of this and following miracles was to do more than relieve physical suffering. If that were the sole purpose, they were insufficient because many were not healed. Rather, the purpose was to draw attention to the one who could cure humankind's most severe affliction, the disfiguring scourge of sin.

First to Preach to the Gentiles

Acts 10

The instruction of Jesus to his apostles previous to their first preaching tour limited them to "the lost sheep of Israel" (Matthew 10:5, 6). When seventy-two evangelists were sent out, no ethnic parameters were stated, but were implied. Jesus said God's judgment would be more tolerable for Gentile cities than for those who refused to hear (Luke 10:1-16). Therefore, it took miraculous direction and revelation for the church to begin to reach out to Gentiles.

I. **GOD SUPERNATURALLY PREPARED HEARTS AND MINDS FOR THE INCLUSION OF GENTILES INTO THE KINGDOM.**
   A. Cornelius was prepared by God to be the first Gentile Christian (Acts 10:1-8).
      1. He was a centurion, a respected Roman commander over one hundred soldiers stationed at Caesarea.
      2. He was also a man of some spiritual stature—devout, God-fearing, benevolent, and prayerful.
      3. God provided a vision in which Cornelius distinctly saw an angel. The angel told him to send for Peter who was residing by the sea at Joppa.

   B. Peter was prepared by God to be the first to bring the gospel to Gentiles (vv. 9-16).
      1. It was about noon when Peter went on the housetop to pray—not the normal time of 3:00 P.M. for prayer.
      2. The lunch hour must have been similar to ours. Peter was hungry.
      3. God caused Peter's mind to be put into a trance and supplied a vision to reveal his will to Peter.
      4. Even entranced, Peter found the content to be so revolting that he argued with God's direct command to him.
      5. It took three replays of the vision to get Peter to obey.
      6. Both Cornelius and Peter recognized that the entire four-day-long episode was the Lord's doings (vv. 22, 23, 28).

II. **PETER FAITHFULLY RESPONDED TO GOD'S DIRECTIVES.**
   A. Peter proclaimed Jesus as "Lord of all" (v. 36).
      1. This is probably a reference to the Hebrew title, "Lord of Sabaoth." This title is found twice in the New Testament, in Romans 9:29 (KJV) and in James 5:4 (KJV).

2. The title does not mean "Lord of the Sabbath," but rather, "Lord of hosts." Great numbers of people are implied.
3. Though some translate "Lord of Sabaoth" as "the Lord Almighty," such a translation misses the implication of the title. The context in both New Testament references is not stressing the strength and power of God but rather his love and mercy for all. James argues that Lord of Sabaoth loves both the rich and the poor. In Romans, Paul reasons that Lord of Sabaoth saves both Jew and Gentile by grace.
4. Peter concurs here, proclaiming Jesus as Lord of the masses.

B. Peter clearly outlined the essentials of the gospel to the many who had gathered at the home of Cornelius (vv. 37-43).
1. Jesus was anointed with the Holy Spirit and with power. This is equivalent to saying he was God's Messiah.
2. Jesus went about doing good, healing the devil's captives.
3. Jesus was crucified.
4. God raised Jesus from the dead.
5. Jesus was appointed by God to be the judge of the living and dead (v. 42).
6. Jesus fulfilled all that the prophets wrote concerning him.
7. Remission of sin is granted through Jesus to believers.

C. The coming of the Holy Spirit interrupted and authenticated Peter's sermon (vv. 44-46).
1. The believing Jews were amazed because Gentiles were blessed just as the apostles had been on Pentecost. The crowd gathered at Cornelius's house spoke in tongues and gave glory to God.
2. Peter later reported the incident was like that of the apostles "at the beginning" (Acts 11:15-17).

D. Peter rationally responded to this further action of God by baptizing the Gentile believers in the name of Jesus (vv. 47, 48).

CONCLUSION

Peter broke through personal prejudice, social convention, and religious dogma by preaching to Gentiles. He was fulfilling the Great Commission, reaching out to "all nations" (Matthew 28:19). God still calls for obedient disciples to venture beyond their comfort zones today.

First Death Row Inmate Miraculously Released

Acts 12

It has been said that the apostles had inside information about prisons all the way from Jerusalem to Rome. This arrest record began after the healing of the lame man, when Peter's preaching had offended the Sadducees. Evidence of a resurrected Savior conflicted with that sect's disbelief in life after death (Acts 4:1-3). Theirs was a minority theological opinion, however, so they were not able to overcome the positive publicity generated by the remarkable miracle (Acts 4:21). Even when their authority was directly snubbed, the Sadducees knew that they could not muster support for the apostles' execution (5:27-40).

But the popular tide seemed to turn against the apostles after Gentiles were admitted to the church. Herod's execution of James bar Zebedee "pleased the Jews" (12:3). An emboldened Herod arrested Peter and sentenced him to die. While Peter was on "death row," three factors contributed to history's most sensational jailbreak.

I. THE CHURCH PRAYED.

A. They prayed "earnestly" (v. 5).

1. Peter slept, but the church was wide awake, praying.
2. The church expected that Peter would be dead the next day.
3. Sincere and honest heart desire is always essential for answered prayer.

B. They prayed in unity (v. 12).

1. One can only conjecture about the number gathered at Mary's home. Whatever the number, they prayed as one.
2. They were united in Christ, in spirit, and in desire.

C. They prayed specifically for Peter (v. 5).

1. There were no vain repetitions in that prayer meeting. No one was concerned about flowery language.
2. It is probable that different specific requests were made. Surely they prayed that Peter's life might be spared. Some may have prayed that he be faithful and not deny his Lord. Probably some requested that Peter would be a powerful witness for Christ at the prison. Still others may have told God how much Peter was needed in the church.

II. GOD EXERCISED HIS SOVEREIGNTY.

A. Man's extremity is God's opportunity.

1. Herod was on the throne. He was typical of all the Herods. The Herod ruling when Jesus was born was grandfather to the Herod Agrippa of our text. The Herod who ordered the beheading of John the Baptist was uncle to the Herod in this text. Claudius, the emperor who preceded Nero on the throne at Rome, would have turned a deaf ear to an appeal by Christians to overturn Herod's decision.
2. The Christians had no other recourse than an appeal to God.

B. God answers prayer.
1. He sent an angel and a bright light to awaken Peter (v. 7).
2. Chains binding Peter were caused to fall off (v. 7).
3. Guards were blinded to the escape (v. 10).
4. The gate of the prison opened without human hands (v. 10).
5. "Stone walls do not a prison make" when God's people pray and God enters the arena of human affairs.

III. PETER RESPONDED WITH OBEDIENCE.

A. Answered prayers hinge upon obedient action.
1. Man is to pray as if all depends upon God and to work as if all depends upon man.
2. Unanswered prayers are frequently all mouth; feet must be put on answered prayer.

B. Peter complied with a number of orders (vv. 7-9).
1. "Quick, get up!" When God calls we must awaken.
2. "Put on your clothes and sandals." At God's call we must be prepared for travel.
3. "Wrap your cloak around you." God may call us to go outside of the box in which we live. Are we prepared for the "chill" that often greets us in the world?
4. "Follow me." Peter had no qualms about this. He followed, even though he did not fully understand his situation. Are we willing to act upon God's commands in faith, even before our minds comprehend his plans?

CONCLUSION

Peter's escape is a beautiful illustration of every believer's deliverance from the death sentence sin brings. God alone brings salvation. Each individual must respond in faith, accepting God's gift. The church witnesses the display of God's power and prays for more escapees.

Peter's Reflections Upon Jesus

1 Peter

Scholars claim that apart from the Gospels one could know the person of Jesus through the epistles of Paul. That claim being true, how much more should we expect to learn about Jesus in the epistles written by Peter? While Paul received the facts of the gospel through supernatural revelation (Galatians 1:11, 12), Peter learned in the "traveling university" as he walked with Jesus for more than three years. When we survey Peter's first letter, we get glimpses of the Savior that match the portraits painted in the Gospels.

I. PETER REFLECTED UPON JESUS' CHARACTER (1 PETER 2:21-23).

A. Jesus exemplified a life of righteousness, even in the face of suffering (v. 22).

1. "He committed no sin."
2. "No deceit was found in his mouth."
3. In both words and deeds Jesus demonstrated a character of righteousness, leaving us an example to follow.

B. Jesus exemplified a life of trust, even in the face of injustice (v. 23).

1. "When they hurled their insults at him, he did not retaliate; when he suffered, he made no threats."
2. "Instead, he entrusted himself to him who judges justly."
3. Jesus knew he did not need to threaten nor retaliate, knowing that God is both just and sovereign.

II. PETER REFLECTED UPON JESUS' SACRIFICIAL DEATH.

A. Jesus' death is part of God's plan (1:10-12, 20).

1. "He was chosen before the creation of the world."
2. His death was predicted by the prophets.

B. Jesus' death is substitutionary.

1. Jesus' life was substituted for ours for the sake of punishment. The righteous one assumed the debt of the unrighteous ones (3:18).
2. Jesus' values should now be substituted for our fleshly desires as we live. We are to assume the goals of our Savior and live for righteousness rather than to satisfy our fallen nature (2:24).

III. PETER REFLECTED UPON JESUS' RESURRECTION.

A. Jesus' resurrection allows him to continue his ministry of preaching through the agency of the Holy Spirit to those dead in sin (3:18, 19; John 16:5-11).

B. Jesus' resurrection cleanses us from sin, an act depicted in the practice of baptism (1 Peter 3:21).

IV. PETER REFLECTED UPON JESUS' GLORIFICATION.

A. Jesus' glorification affirms the justice of God by restoring one sentenced as a criminal to his rightful position.
   1. God planned that the glorification of the Christ would follow the suffering of Jesus (1:11; Hebrews 12:2).
   2. Though he was "rejected by men," as demonstrated in his suffering, he was "chosen by God and precious to him," as demonstrated by his glorification (1 Peter 2:4).

B. Jesus' glorification assures that his authority will be recognized by all.
   1. Heavenly powers now submit to him (3:22).
   2. All of heaven and earth are subject to him and will one day be graphically demonstrated (Philippians 2:9-11). When Jesus comes again, his glory will be revealed and men's joy will overflow (1 Peter 1:7; 4:13).

ILLUSTRATIONS

Trusting God to right injustice. Eva went to the door to see what a noisy ruckus in the yard was all about. She stood silent to appraise the circumstances and saw her son put his arm around a little buddy, leading him away from the fray and comforting his friend saying, "Vengeance are mine, saith the Lord." His grammar was not so good but his theology was excellent.

Recognizing Jesus' authority. Mr. Russell did all possible to oppose anything religious and keep his daughter from attending church services. The first time I called at his home to witness for Christ he raised his hand high toward Heaven and said, "If there is a God let him strike me dead right now." I later crossed paths with Mr. Russell at a garage where I went to witness to the proprietor. Parts of a carburetor in his hand which he was attempting to assemble slipped and flew apart. Mr. Russell said, "That would make a preacher swear." He continued with crude diatribe. I told him that someday, whether he wanted to or not, he would open his mouth and confess that Jesus was Lord and the Son of God. I baptized the owner of the garage. Russell's daughter attended Bible college and I officiated at her marriage to a preacher. I often wonder what happened to Mr. Russell.

The Salutations

1 Peter 1:1, 2; 5:13; 2 Peter 1:1

Letter writers of Peter's day had a relatively standard form to their salutations. Letters ranging from royal pronouncements to common social notes regularly included three elements. Those elements were information concerning the author, a description of the recipients, and a meaningful greeting. Looking at these three elements in Peter's epistles will aid our understanding of the content of these epistles.

I. **PETER CLAIMED TO BE WRITING FROM "BABYLON" (1 PETER 5:13).**

   A. Peter may have been writing from Babylon on the Euphrates. The ancient city, however, had been long destroyed and was of little significance in the first century. Nevertheless, there may have been Jews and proselytes there (Acts 2:9).

   B. Another Babylon in existence at the time was a small community a short distance from Cairo, Egypt. This village was primarily a fort where Roman soldiers were quartered. For that reason, few Jews, if any, would be attracted there.

   C. Babylon is most likely a figurative reference to Rome.
   1. Rome is referred to as "Babylon" in Jewish literature of the late first century A.D. Such references are found in the Sibylline Oracles, the Apocalypse of Baruch, and Second Esdras.
   2. The apostle John also seems to refer to Rome as Babylon in the book of Revelation (14:8; 16:19; 17:5; 18:2).

II. **THE RECIPIENTS ARE IDENTIFIED AS CHRISTIANS IN THE PROVINCES OF ASIA MINOR (1 PETER 1:1, 2).**

   A. The provinces into which Christians had been scattered are listed in the order one would travel from east to west. Some suggest that Peter had probably just traversed that route on his way to Rome.

   B. Though they are scattered throughout the world, they are united in a common faith.

1. They have been "chosen according to the foreknowledge of God" (1 Peter 1:2).
2. They have "received a faith . . . [that is] . . . precious" (2 Peter 1:1).
3. The Christians to whom Peter writes were in the provinces evangelized by Paul on his missionary tours.

III. THE GREETINGS CONTAIN KERNELS OF TRUTH ABOUT THE CHURCH, JESUS, AND CHURCH LEADERSHIP.

A. Both epistles open with two significant words of greeting—grace and peace.
  1. Gentiles greeted one another with the salutation, "Grace," while Jews addressed each other saying, "Peace to you." This compound greeting is appropriate for the universal church. It joins together the greetings of both Jews and Gentiles.
  2. In both letters Peter's express desire is that "Grace and peace be yours in abundance." Only the Prince of Peace could fulfill that prayer.

B. Peter affirms the deity of Christ in his greetings (2 Peter 1:1, 2).
  1. Jesus and God are a conjoint source of righteousness.
  2. They are also a joint source of grace and peace.

C. In both letters Peter claims personal identity with Jesus.
  1. He refers to himself as a "servant" in the second epistle, but his loving, servant heart is clearly reflected throughout the first epistle.
  2. He also refers to himself as an "apostle," one chosen, commissioned, and empowered by Jesus.

Peter's View of the Trinity

1 Peter 1:2

Though the word "Trinity" is not found in the Bible, the truth of one God existing in three persons is found from Genesis to Revelation. Other religions teach about a plurality of gods, but only Christianity teaches a plurality in unity.

In the first words of his first letter, Peter speaks of all three persons of the Godhead. Each person of the Trinity, Peter teaches, has a unique role in the salvation of mankind.

I.   GOD IN HIS FOREKNOWLEDGE PLANS TO SAVE US.

A. What foreknowledge is

1. God's foreknowledge is complete, spanning the ages from "before the creation of the world" to "last times" (1 Peter 1:20).
2. God's foreknowledge is moral, knowing what is and what will bring about "good." (See Romans 8:28.)
3. God's foreknowledge is unlimited by geography. Though his people are "scattered" (1 Peter 1:1) throughout the known world, he knows each one. God knows who will "elect" to serve him before they make the choice. When they elect, God responds in kind.
4. God's foreknowledge is not limited by time. "A day is like a thousand years, and a thousand years are like a day" (2 Peter 3:8). He not only sees the past of those "called" and "justified," but he sees them in the future as those "glorified." In God's knowledge the entire process of salvation is already complete (Romans 8:29).

B. What foreknowledge is not

1. Foreknowledge should not be equated with cause.
2. God could predict as in all the prophecies of his Word on the basis of his omniscience. He knew his predictions would come to pass, but he was not the primary cause.
3. God, in his sovereign will, created man with free will. God will never violate his own creation of free moral agency in man.

II. THE HOLY SPIRIT SANCTIFIES US, SETTING APART TO SERVE GOD.

A. Sanctification is a gift.

31

1. Sanctification is an act of grace and can be granted by God alone. Only God can sanctify us, make us holy.
2. If one is a Christian he has been sanctified. The guilt of sin is removed by God upon our conversion. In 1 Corinthians 6:9-11 Paul catalogues sins in which the Corinthians had previously been involved. Then he states "you were sanctified." The Greek text indicates a completed act in which the recipient is passive. God is the one acting.

B. Sanctification is also a growth process.
1. With the past wholly erased through divine sanctification, the Christian begins the process of growth in holiness.
2. Christians are to grow in the grace and knowledge of our Lord Jesus Christ (2 Peter 3:18). They add virtues to their sanctified lives (2 Peter 1:5-8).

C. We can refuse to let sanctification be effective in our lives.
1. When Peter says that we can keep from being "ineffective and unproductive" in our lives for God "if" we accept the qualities of holiness he desires we have, Peter is assuming a choice on our part.
2. We are not promised that the Holy Spirit will ever make us wholly immune to sin. There is no such doctrine as a "second work of grace" in the Scriptures.

III.   THE BLOOD OF JESUS PAYS THE PRICE FOR OUR SALVATION.

A. Old Testament sacrifices were continual. Blood needed to be regularly shed to roll back the guilt of sin (Hebrews 9:19-22).

B. Jesus provided a "new and living way." His one-time sacrifice permanently removes the sin barrier between God and humanity (Hebrews 10:19-23).

ILLUSTRATION

Our salvation is initiated by God, not ourselves. Every day for six weeks while residing in a guest house in Chiangmai, Thailand, I was awakened by the owner tinkling his bell, taking fish, meat, or flowers to his little worship center in the corner of the tennis court, hoping to get his god to smile upon him that day.

The sacrifice of Jesus was foreshadowed when *Jehovah Jireh,* God the provider, supplied the ram to be offered in the place of Isaac. This is a major difference from all pagan religions that require the worshiper to provide the sacrifice which he hopes will secure the good will of the deities.

Saved Yesterday, Today, and Tomorrow

1 Peter 1:3-12

Sometimes Christians are embarrassed to answer the question, "Are you saved?" They fear a positive answer will appear to be self-righteous. Peter's discussion of salvation as being past, present, and future should provide a ready answer to that most significant question.

I. SALVATION IS FUTURE (vv. 3-5).

A. New birth provides a living hope.
  1. Hope always speaks of the future.
  2. This hope is based upon the resurrection of Jesus. Paul agrees (1 Corinthians 15:12-19).

B. An inheritance awaits those who are saved.
  1. It is imperishable. Salvation is the treasure of which Jesus spoke in the Sermon on the Mount (Matthew 6:19, 20).
  2. It is reserved in Heaven for those who in faith commit themselves into God's protective care.

C. It is a salvation ready to be revealed in the last time.
  1. In God's mind it is ready and there will be no delays. It will occur just as the lightning flashes east to west.
  2. That supreme moment will be unexpected by men, like when a home is invaded by a thief (2 Peter 3:10).
  3. A new Heaven and earth will provide both re-creation and restitution of humankind (2 Peter 3:11, 12).
  4. Those who have put on the righteousness of Christ will find a "home of righteousness" there (2 Peter 3:13).

II. SALVATION IS PRESENT (vv. 6-9).

A. It is the source of rejoicing in everyday life.
  1. Joy and happiness characterize the Christian life (Philippians 3:1; 4:4).
  2. Rejoicing is possible even in the face of all kinds of trials. First Peter was probably written as Neronian persecution against Christians had spent its terrible force and was waning. Paul was beheaded in 67 A.D., and Peter was crucified in 68 A.D.

3. The "little while" of suffering is relative. Contrast it with the millennia of time or even with eternity.

4. Faith is proven to be genuine by remaining firm in trials.

B. Christians are receiving right now the goal of their faith which is salvation.

III. SALVATION IS PAST (vv. 10-12).

A. Salvation was prophesied, but not fully understood.

1. The prophets were still asking the big questions—Who? What? When?
2. The sufferings of Christ were predicted, but even Peter did not understand those predictions (Matthew 16:21-23).

B. The prophets' words were explained by the gospel. The Old Testament was the foundation; the New Testament was the superstructure. The Old Testament was the booster; the New Testament was the missile.

C. Even angels longed for information.

1. What did they think when Jesus left Heaven? What did they think of the agonies of Calvary? What did they think when he returned to glory?
2. Angels could not learn of salvation by personal experience. They are not saved (Hebrews 2:16).
3. It is only through the church that God's plan of redemption for man was made known to those in the "heavenly realms" (Ephesians 3:10).
4. Angels could only learn gradually as God's plan unfolded.

CONCLUSION

How does one answer the question, "Are you saved?" According to Peter, our answer is clear: "I have been, I am being, and I shall be saved!"

The Transformed Life

1 Peter 1:13-25

After writing about the blessings of our salvation in 1:3-12, Peter makes a logical conclusion. That conclusion is that blessing and liberty in Christ incur obligations and responsibility. While Christians love to sing the hymn, "Count Your Blessings," perhaps we should add a chorus:

Count your obligations, name them one by one,
And it will surprise you what the Lord wants done.

Peter emphasizes the Christian's proper response to God's love and salvation. It is to live a transformed life. He describes three elements of such a life.

I.   THE TRANSFORMED LIFE LIVES IN OBEDIENCE.

A. We are to be "children of obedience" (v. 14).

1. Although this phrase is translated by some as "obedient children," the original language has a slightly different emphasis. The literal translation, "children of obedience," suggests the idea that Christians are children of their parentage, which is obedience.

2. The exact opposite parental concept is involved in Ephesians 5:6, as Paul refers to "Sons of disobedience."

3. The language seems to suggest that our obedience or lack of obedience gives birth to character.

B. Obedience changes our relationships (v. 22).

1. Obedience brings a greater degree of personal purity.

2. Obedience adds to our sincere love for each other.

II.   THE TRANSFORMED LIFE THINKS WITH A NEW ATTITUDE.

A. Regeneration begins in the mind (v. 13).

1. Faith and repentance involve the mind. While "prepare your minds for action" is an accurate translation, the original language paints a very interesting picture. In the East where long robes were worn, the phrase, "Gird up the loins of your mind," would be very meaningful. Robes were lifted and fastened with a belt about the waist to obtain freedom of movement. We need to gather our thoughts together so they don't trip us up!

2. Alert, careful, determinate action is implied. Peter probably learned this figure of speech from Jesus (Luke 12:35, 36).

B. Reformation of life (repentance) begins in the mind.

    1. Our minds should be "self-controlled" or sober (v. 13). A disciplined life is the opposite of one which is out of control, like someone who is drunk.

    2. The succinct directive of Paul sums it up, "Be transformed by the renewing of your mind" (Romans 12:2).

    3. Christians are not to indulge in former evil practices in which they participated when they lived in ignorance (v. 14).

III. THE TRANSFORMED LIFE IS DIRECTED WITH PROPER GOALS.

A. We must set our hope securely on God's grace (v. 13).

    1. The final demonstration of God's grace will appear when Jesus comes.

    2. He appeared once to "take away the sins of many people." He will appear a second time to save "those who are waiting for him" (Hebrews 9:28). This is God's final act of grace.

B. We must seek to be godlike (vv. 15, 16).

    1. "Be holy, because I am holy." This has been called the grandest apologetic for Christian living.

    2. God's eternal election is to the end that we might be holy. "He chose us in him [Christ] before the creation of the world to be holy and blameless" (Ephesians 1:4).

    3. When one claims to be a child of God but does not live a holy life, he is inadvertently testifying that God either does not exist or that he is not holy.

ILLUSTRATION

The importance of a renewed mind. When visiting my doctor for personal health care, our discussion fumed to moral decadence in American culture. In speaking of sexual conduct and orientation the doctor said, "The most potent and determinative sexual organ all persons possess is right between the ears." The mind dictates, and without it the body is comatose.

Putting Off and Putting On

1 Peter 2:1-3

God's plan to redeem mankind has been unfolding through the centuries and will be fully completed in the return of Christ. We human beings are to respond to God's gracious plan by living a life which demonstrates a thankful response to redemption. In these verses, Peter describes that response with the metaphor of changing clothes. He lists attributes we need to strip from ourselves as well as the attributes in which we must be clothed.

I. **WE MUST STRIP THESE GARMENTS OF SIN FROM OUR LIVES.**

 A. Malice (*kakia*)
   1. This word refers in general to all kinds of evil. This particular reference is to active, destructive ill will.
   2. Lightfoot states that the word indicates "the vicious nature which is bent on doing harm to others."

 B. Deceit (*dolos*)
   1. The word has numerous possible translations: guile, bait, lure, snare, craft.
   2. An Old Testament example is that of Jacob, the supplanter, who abandoned brotherly love and broke proper familial relationship by deceit (Genesis 27).
   3. A positive New Testament example is Nathaniel. Jesus praised the character of Nathaniel by pronouncing him to be "a true Israelite, in whom there is nothing false" (John 1:47).

 C. Hypocrisies (*hupokrisis*)
   1. The word means "pretense" or "playacting."
   2. When one's commitment to truth is only pretense, he or she becomes a dangerous enemy of unity and true brotherhood.
   3. Some of Jesus' strongest words were against those whose religion was "playacting" (Matthew 23).

 D. Envy (*psthonos*)
   1. Envy is jealousy and resentment toward another who is superior in any way. It is the product of a covetous spirit.

37

2. Envy and jealousy motivated the sons of Jacob to sell Joseph into slavery (Genesis 37).
3. Pilate knew that Jesus was delivered up to be crucified because of envy (Matthew 27:18).

E. Slander (*katalalias*)
1. This word is defined as speaking against another to incriminate or defame, the normal function of gossip. It is a compound Greek word coming from *kata*, meaning "behind or in back of" and *lalias*, meaning "to speak." It is "talking behind someone's back"!
2. Paul noted that this negative quality was found in the midst of a number of other negative qualities in the church in Corinth (2 Corinthians 12:20).

II. WE MUST PUT ON POSITIVE TRAITS IN THE ABSENCE OF THOSE NEGATIVE ONES.

A. Newborn Christians must grow in the Lord.
1. Christianity never produces a vacuum. We can never truly be defined by what we are not.
2. Negatives are replaced with positive virtues.

B. Christians must long for spiritual food.
1. Peter indicates that once we have experienced the Lord's blessings, we desire more of the same (v. 3). He is echoing the words of the psalmist, "Taste and see that the Lord is good" (Psalm 34:8).
2. Such is the reasoning of popular TV commercials of years ago: "Try it, you'll like it!" and "Bet you can't eat just one!"

C. The Word of God is our "spiritual milk."
1. The word translated "spiritual" is *logikos*, the source of our English word "logical." It is related to the Greek word, *logos*, meaning "word." (See John 1:1.)
2. The only other time this word is used is in Romans 12:1. Paul says that becoming a living sacrifice for our Savior is our *logikon* (logical, reasonable, spiritual) worship.
3. It is not possible to receive this milk passively, through a "spiritual IV." One must crave and actively consume God's Word.

ILLUSTRATION

Scuttling unnecessary cargo. Crews on board ships in trouble at sea have frequently been willing to throw their entire cargo overboard in an attempt to save their ship and their lives. Note how this was done on Paul's trip to Rome (Acts 27:18, 19). In a figurative sense, Christians need to scuttle negative mental, emotional, and spiritual freight if we are to reach our desired destination.

The Collected Body

1 Peter 2:4-12

Many terms are used in Scripture to identify the church. Some of those are the body of Christ, the temple of the Holy Spirit, the family of God, the kingdom of God, and the bride of Christ. Peter adds two more to that list in this text.

I. THE CHURCH IS A SPIRITUAL HOUSE (vv. 4-8).

A. The foundation of this house is "the living Stone."

   1. Jesus is the mighty rock sheltering a weary land (Isaiah 32:2), the stone cut not with human hands that will conquer human kingdoms (Daniel 2:44, 45). He is the Messiah, chosen by God.
   2. In addition to being "rock solid," our foundation stone is living. The resurrection of Jesus is absolutely essential to our faith. Jesus opened a "new and living way" to God's presence (Hebrews 10:20). Jesus is a "life-giving spirit" (1 Corinthians 15:45).
   3. In unison with the "living Stone" Christians also become living stones.

B. Though Jesus is our foundation stone, he has been rejected by men.

   1. As a mason discards an inferior brick or stone, so Jesus was rejected. "His own did not receive him" (John 1:11).
   2. Jesus predicted his rejection (Mark 8:31).
   3. Peter announced the historic fulfillment of the prediction of Jesus' rejection (Acts 2:36).
   4. A glance at the world today informs us that the rejection is still in progress.

II. THE CHURCH IS A CHOSEN PEOPLE (vv. 9, 10).

A. The church contains people chosen without regard to nationality.

   1. Gentiles are included in God's election and all physical distinctions are erased (Galatians 3:26-29).
   2. Peter's reference to having been "not a people" probably is a reference to Hosea 1:6-9. The names of Hosea's children are prophetic. The prefix "Lo" in Hebrew is negative. *Ruhamah* means "loved, wanted." When the prefix is added (*Loruhamah*) it means "unloved, unwanted." *Ammi* means "my people"; *Loammi*, "no kin of mine." Paul, by inspiration, interpreted this Hosea passage as relating to Jews and Gentiles (Romans 9:25).

3. The Gentiles, with whom God did not covenant at first, were added to those of the blood line of Abraham to become "spiritual Israel" (Galatians 3:14).

B. The church has been chosen to become a royal priesthood.
 1. We are "a kingdom and priests" because we have been liberated by the King of kings (Revelation 1:5, 6).
 2. The basic function of a priest is to intercede, to be a bridge. In the patriarchal dispensation the father offered sacrifices on behalf of his family. (See Job 1:5.) In the Mosaic dispensation the priesthood was limited to the tribe of Levi and the family of Aaron. As a nation Israel should have made intercession between God and all the nations of the world, but became introverted and failed (Exodus 19:6).
 3. With Christ as our high priest, Christians are all responsible to reach out to the world with a view to closing the tremendous gulf between God and sinners.

C. The church's job is to "declare the praises" of God (vv. 9, 11, 12).
 1. God's first chosen, Israel, failed to bring praise to him, and a sad criticism is leveled against them. "God's name is blasphemed among the Gentiles because of you" (Romans 2:24).
 2. The church must be what God intended her to be in order to bring praise to him. She has been called "out of darkness into his wonderful light."
 3. Therefore, Christians must walk in the light. We must "abstain from sinful desires," "live . . . good lives among the pagans," and "glorify God."

Proper Relationship to Authority

1 Peter 2:11-21

Christians in this world are "aliens and strangers." That description carries the concept of a condition which is temporary and no legal rights or status have been obtained. This is because the Christian's citizenship is in Heaven (Philippians 3:20). We are like God's servants of old who "admitted that they were aliens and strangers on earth" (Hebrews 11:13).

As those without authority of our own, we Christians must submit to those to whom authority has been granted in this world. Peter argues that by showing respect to earthly leaders, we display the qualities of our Heavenly Leader.

I. **CHRISTIAN CITIZENS MUST RESPECT GOVERNMENT AUTHORITY (vv. 13-17).**
    A. Peter exhorted the readers of his letter to obey the king and his governors. Today that would certainly apply to federal, state, and local authorities.
        1. We are to obey "for the Lord's sake." These human authorities are "sent by him."
        2. The word translated "authority" in the first part of verse 13 is the Greek word *ktisis*. This word is reserved exclusively in the New Testament for the activity and products of God. It is the same word which is translated "creation" in Romans 8:18-20. Governmental authority is a creation of God and those who ignore this fact will answer to God (Romans 13:1-7).

    B. God instituted government to control the bent of humanity's sinful nature.
        1. Government is to punish the evildoers and commend and encourage those who are righteous.
        2. Obviously God's desire is for man to live orderly and securely.

    C. Christian obedience to authority silences slanderous accusations against the church.
        1. Pagans in the early days of the church accused Christians of many outrageous acts including infanticide and eating babies in sacred meals.
        2. Today many accuse Christians of outrageous acts such as racism and the domination of women.
        3. When the world sees believers being "model citizens," both ancient and modern accusations lose credibility.

41

D. Christians rejoice in their freedom in Christ, but should never use their freedom to excuse rebellion.

    1. Christians should be willing to go beyond that which authority requires. (See Matthew 5:41.)

    2. Christians "do good to all people" (Galatians 6:10), love the church, and honor all rulers.

    3. Above all, they should reverence God (Acts 4:19; 5:28, 29).

II. CHRISTIAN EMPLOYEES MUST RESPECT THEIR BOSSES (vv. 18-21).

A. Employees owe a proper respect and response to their employers.

    1. This is not limited to those employers who are easy to please.

    2. In times of difficulty, Christian employees need to be more conscious of God than they are of the circumstances around them.

B. Christ, the perfect one, left the example.

    1. He was insulted but did not retaliate. He threatened no one.

    2. He accepted suffering for others who are healed by his wounds. (See Isaiah 53:1-12.)

CONCLUSION

Jesus has granted us freedom now. He will grant us authority in the age to come (1 Corinthians 6:3). Yet in this age, none of us are "high and mighty." We are like sheep who have gone astray and turned to the Good Shepherd to meet our needs. With this humble attitude of submission we will win a hearing from others.

Wives and Husbands

1 Peter 3:1-7

The relationship of husband and wife reaches back to the dawn of time. Marital life is pictured throughout Scripture with amazing objectivity. Strengths and weaknesses, victories and failures are all described with no window dressing.

Today, many attempt to redefine the words "marriage" and "family." In this text, Peter outlines the behaviors that make the God-ordained marriage relationship work.

I. DUTIES OF WIVES IN MARRIAGE (vv. 1-6).

A. Wives are to submit to their husbands.

1. Peter's choice of vocabulary here is the compound Greek word *hupotasso*. *Hupo* means under. The verb *tasso* means "to place in a certain order." Peter instructs wives to place themselves under the authority of their husbands.

2. Power struggles are inevitable in human relationships. In any interaction, someone must have the final say. Rather than have dominance be determined by conflict, a wife can make a preemptive strike by placing herself under her husband's leadership.

3. Although this idea of submission is almost totally rejected by the world, it is clearly the pattern taught in Scripture. Peter points to this attitude present in "the holy women of the past," including Sarah, the wife of Abraham (vv. 5, 6).

4. Peter recognizes that the biggest roadblock to this attitude is that the woman "give way to fear," presumably the fear of placing too much control of her life outside of her own hands.

B. Wives are to display "purity and reverence."

1. Outward beauty fades but not the "beauty of a gentle and quiet spirit" (v. 4).

2. It is inner strength and virtue which lead the non-Christian husband to Christ (vv. 1, 2).

3. This passage does not issue a total ban on jewelry, cosmetics, and fine clothes. After all, the Old Testament describes the virtuous wife as being "clothed in fine linen and purple" (Proverbs 31:22). Extremes in jewelry, garb, and cosmetics that distract attention from true inner beauty should be avoided.

43

II. DUTIES OF HUSBANDS IN MARRIAGE (v. 7)

A. Because they have been given authority in marriage, husbands have the responsibility to treat wives in a way which they know to be right.

1. The phrase translated "considerate" is *kata gnosis*, which literally means "according to knowledge."

2. Husbands should know better than to treat their wives with disrespect. In a modern vernacular Peter is saying, "Husbands, don't even THINK about mistreating your wives!"

B. The wife is to be treated as the weaker partner.

1. The weakness alluded to here is probably not a reference to genetic weakness of any sort. Peter is not saying that men have innate superiority of any sort to women.

2. Rather, Peter is making a reference to the above-mentioned power difference. In other words, Peter is again warning the husband not to misuse his authority in marriage.

C. Husbands are to recognize their wives are joint-heirs of God's gracious gift of life.

1. In his discussion of the marriage relationship, Paul also commands that wives submit to their husbands. In addition, however, he notes that submission is mutual. Wives submit to the authority of their husbands, while husbands subjugate their personal needs to those of their wives (Ephesians 5:21-33). It is this mutuality to which Peter refers also.

2. Failure to be responsible for the needs of his wife causes a break in communication between the husband and God.

CONCLUSION

Marriage and the family are foundational institutions of the human race. Because of the importance of these relationships, God chose not to be silent on the issue. In his grace he provides clear teaching about the behaviors necessary for successful unions. We ignore his words at our own risk.

ILLUSTRATION

Won without words. My early home was on a farm near Kimball, Minnesota. Mother told me that my father was kind and considerate of her in most respects. He was glad to hitch up the horse and buggy for Mom to shop or attend some social function of the neighborhood. He refused to do the same when Mother wanted to attend church. To do so she had to hitch Topsy to the buggy herself. Dad knew how important her faith in Christ was by her willingness to do just that. He became a Christian at the age of 46. Other factors influenced my father, but at rock bottom was the influence of his wife. I'm so glad my mother was that kind of wife.

Suffering as a Christian

1 Peter 3:13–4:6

Peter's letter was written to comfort suffering Christians. At that time, the Roman emperor Nero was savagely attacking Christians in Rome. History tells us that both Paul and Peter eventually died in this persecution. Despite knowledge of this vicious offensive, Peter writes about how God can use it for his purposes.

I. **CHRISTIANS ARE CALLED TO SUFFER FOR THE SAKE OF RIGHTEOUSNESS (3:13, 14).**
   A. While those who live righteously usually will not suffer at the hands of government authority, at times there are exceptions.
   1. Our Lord is the supreme example.
   2. The Holocaust during World War II is a well-known example of extreme religious persecution in the twentieth century.
   3. Though less widely-publicized, Christians are targets of physical attack yet today in parts of the Middle East and Far East.

   B. We cannot control the attitudes and actions of those who persecute. We can only control our reaction to persecution.
   1. We can understand that we are being persecuted because our faith is recognized as being authentic. (See Matthew 5:10-12; John 15:18, 19.)
   2. We must resist being intimidated. Persecution is an attempt to force idolatry upon us. Persecutors want believers to fear them rather than God.
   3. If one must suffer it is better to do so for right rather than for wrong.

II. **CHRISTIANS ARE CALLED TO BEAR WITNESS TO JESUS EVEN IN THE MIDST OF SUFFERING (3:15, 16).**
   A. We are called to be true to the Lordship of Christ even when we are in physical danger.
   1. We need to be prepared to make a reasonable defense of our faith at any time in any circumstances. The Greek word for "answer" is *apologia*, from where we get the word "apologetics," the discipline of logically defending one's beliefs.
   2. Early Christians were called before magistrates and courts (Mark 13:9; Acts 7). Their duty in such circumstances was to defend their faith, not themselves.

B. We are called to speak with meekness, gentleness, and respect, even in these stressful circumstances.

1. The only bit of information Jesus volunteered in reference to his personal character was "I am meek and lowly in heart" (Matthew 11:29, KJV).
2. Every sincere Christian knows that he has nothing to brag about and is humbled by God's plan. An oft leveled criticism against Christians is that they think they are better than others.
3. Believers must live so that they will not be ashamed of their lives. A believer's life should never contradict his or her verbal witness. In fact, our lives should be so consistent that our critics should be embarrassed by trying to find fault with us.

III. CHRISTIANS ARE CALLED TO LET SUFFERING PRODUCE FRUIT (4:1-6).

A. The potential for suffering encourages us to take life and faith seriously.

1. We are to arm ourselves with a Christ-like attitude. Like Jesus, we are to live life with intention, purpose, and resolution.
2. Early Christians knew their faith was serious business. They faced Jewish persecution, Roman opposition, and mob action.
3. Today our faith remains serious business. We need to prepare for today's spiritual battles (Ephesians 6:10-18) and for today's ethical battles (Romans 13:12-14).

B. The potential for suffering encourages us to prioritize what we value.

1. That which is worth suffering for is worth living for. Earthly things and desires of the flesh lose their charm.
2. We can thank God for suffering if it is an aid in overcoming sin. Both the wicked and the righteous must give account for the things done in this life (2 Corinthians 5:9, 10).

ILLUSTRATION

Persecution of believers today. We taught at a family camp on the shore of the Mediterranean, near Alexandria, Egypt. A government soldier sat daily at the gate to the camp in camouflage garb with an automatic gun across his lap. He was protecting Christians. About that same time many Christians were mowed down by gunfire as they came out from their Sunday assembly.

Preaching to the Spirits in Prison (Part 1)

1 Peter 3:18-22

Some portions of Scripture are especially difficult to understand. This "mysterious passage" is one of the most confusing of all. Scholars have modified their exegesis of this text more frequently than any other in the New Testament.

Three major views have been proposed to explain what Peter meant by saying Jesus "went and preached to the spirits in prison." Two will be addressed in this sermon.

I. THE PASSAGE COULD BE INTERPRETED METAPHORICALLY.

A. Christ was the "Spirit" who motivated Noah to preach.

  1. In other words, Peter may have simply been saying that the message of repentance and salvation preached by Noah was a different part of the same gospel completed in Jesus.

  2. This is similar to what Paul was saying to the Corinthians when he compared the rock from which water flowed to quench the thirsts of the Israelites in the desert to Christ (1 Corinthians 10:1-4).

B. If Noah were the preacher, then he was preaching to the men and women who were living upon the earth just before the flood.

  1. The preaching would probably be about his orders to build an ark and the predicted flood.

  2. The prison in which the spirits were held (v. 19) would refer to the bodies of men and their sins. It should be noted, however, that the word "prison" is singular in the Greek.

  3. A major difficulty with this view is to explain why Peter would leave the thought of Christ's suffering and death and jump thousands of years to an incident which has no bearing upon his theme. The message of salvation is present in the story of Noah, so this interpretation would be sensible if Peter were simply talking about redemption. Nevertheless, in the context of this passage Peter was talking about Jesus' suffering. It is unclear how Jesus' suffering is found in the story of Noah.

II. THE PASSAGE COULD BE INTERPRETED IN ITS MOST LITERAL SENSE.

A. Jesus went to the dwelling place of the dead to preach to the spirits of people who died during the flood of Noah.

1. Those holding this position would say that the event occurred between the time of the crucifixion and the resurrection.
2. While Jesus' body was in the tomb of Joseph of Arimathea, his spirit was in the abode of the dead. There he preached to those who rejected Noah's message.

B. Bible passages referring to the abode of the dead before the resurrection of Christ refer to all people who have died being in Sheol (Hebrew) or Hades (Greek) (Psalm 16:10; Acts 2:27).
1. Most translations translate Sheol and Hades as "the grave."
2. First Samuel 28:19 indicates that a righteous prophet and a wicked king (both the wicked and righteous sons) would be together in the abode of the dead. First Samuel 31:8-13 makes it clear that Samuel was not speaking of the grave in 28:19.
3. In the story of the rich man and Lazarus, Jesus indicates that the righteous and wicked in the abode of the dead are separated by a great gulf but communication is possible (Luke 16:19-31).

C. This interpretation also has significant problems, however.
1. It suggests a second chance or some such concept as purgatory. Some would answer by saying that this preaching was preaching for the purpose of conversion. Peter does not use the Greek word *euaggelizo*, meaning to "preach the good news," but rather *kerusso*, which simply means to "proclaim or announce." The word *kerusso*, however, is often used in the New Testament to indicate preaching for the purpose of conversion (Acts 8:5; Romans 10:14, 15; 1 Corinthians 1:23).
2. This interpretation also fails to explain why Jesus went to the abode of the dead to preach only to the disobedient in the days of Noah. Why not preach to the disobedient of every age?

CONCLUSION

There are many "mystery" passages in Scripture. While they are interesting to study, they may not be able to be fully explained. These passages, however, are the exception to the rule. Most of the Bible's message is no mystery at all. God has designed a loving plan for the salvation of man through the death, burial, and resurrection of his Son.

Preaching to the Spirits in Prison (Part 2)

1 Peter 3:18-22

The preceding sermon surveyed two major attempts to explain this mysterious passage of Scripture. We have looked at a literal interpretation. This view holds that while Jesus' body was in the tomb, his spirit descended to the abode of the dead to preach to those who perished in the great flood. We have examined a metaphorical interpretation which states that Peter's reference was simply a figure of speech. In this view, Peter was saying that the Holy Spirit has proclaimed the message of salvation by grace even in the earliest days of human history.

A third interpretation also exists. This view argues that "spirits in prison" refers to fallen angels. After conquering death, Jesus proclaimed his victory over evil and its minions. Let's examine this view which holds that Christ was making a proclamation to disobedient heavenly spirits, that is, fallen angels.

I. **WHEN THE BIBLE USES THE WORD "SPIRITS," IT USUALLY REFERS TO SUPERNATURAL BEINGS.**
    A. When the word "spirit" is used to refer to human beings in the New Testament, it always appears with a definitive qualifying phrase.
    1. Hebrews 12:23 speaks of "spirits of righteous men made perfect."
    2. Paul states that the "spirits of prophets are subject to the control of prophets" (1 Corinthians 14:32).

    B. The word "spirits" is used regularly in the New Testament of supernatural beings both good and bad.
    1. "Are not all angels ministering spirits sent to serve those who will inherit salvation?" (Hebrews 1:14).
    2. After the seventy-two returned from being sent out by Jesus, they reported that demons submitted to them in the name of Jesus. Jesus replied, "However, do not rejoice that the spirits submit to you, but rejoice that your names are written in heaven" (Luke 10:20).

II. **JEWISH TRADITION AND SCRIPTURE SHED LIGHT UPON THE ORIGIN AND NATURE OF DEMONS.**
    A. It is generally agreed that demons came into being when angels rebelled against God's authority.

1. Josephus and a few other Jewish scholars taught that demons were spirits of wicked men who died. This view is held by a limited minority. Most tradition teaches that demons are fallen angels.
2. Bible scholars generally agree that John was referring to the origin of demons when he said Satan "swept a third of the stars [angels] out of the sky and flung them to the earth" (Revelation 12:4). John continues in that passage to speak of the war between "Michael and his angels" and "the dragon [Satan] and his angels" (Revelation 12:7-9).

B. The original language of the Bible supports the concept that angels do not continue to fall.
1. Peter refers to God's judgment on angels "when they sinned" (2 Peter 2:4). The Greek phrase points to completed action, supporting the position that angels fell at a time in the past and do not continue to fall.
2. Jude refers to "angels who did not keep their positions of authority but abandoned their own home" (Jude 6). Again, the Greek grammar refers to action completed at a point in time in the past.

C. Jewish tradition taught that angels who fell did so before the flood of Noah.
1. Tradition held that those angels who successfully passed through a time of probation, creation to the flood, would never fall.
2. Perhaps Peter and his original audience were familiar with this tradition, hence the reference to the ark in this passage (1 Peter 3:20).

III. **WE CAN INFER THE CONTENT OF THE PREACHING TO THE SPIRITS IN PRISON.**
A. We can assume that the message to the angels was not evangelistic.
1. Angels are not saved (Hebrews 2:12-16).
2. Each angel is wholly, individually responsible for any deviation from the will of God.

B. The proclamation was based upon Christ's victory over sin and death.
1. The judgment of fallen angels was announced by Jesus and was sealed by his authority. They must suffer the consequences of rebellion against God and evil influence among men.
2. Peter seems to stress this in the closing verse of the text, "angels, authorities and powers in submission to him" (1 Peter 3:22).
3. Paul states the same truth. He says when Christ triumphed on the cross he "disarmed the powers and authorities" (Colossians 2:15). When Jesus died, demonic powers were limited.

Gospel Preached to the Dead

1 Peter 4:6

Preaching is one essential in God's program of salvation. One cannot hear the message without a preacher (Romans 10:14), because God ordains that people be won through "the foolishness of preaching" (1 Corinthians 1:21, KJV).

In the fourth chapter of 1 Peter we come upon another difficult passage of Scripture. After announcing that God will judge the living and the dead, Peter declares that the gospel was preached to the dead. Let us examine four ways scholars have explained this passage.

I. **PETER MAY BE REFERRING TO PEOPLE WHO HAD BECOME CHRISTIANS IN PAST YEARS BUT WHO HAD DIED BY THE TIME PETER WROTE.**

    A. The church had been in existence three decades at the time of this writing.

        1. Many who had become believers in the earlier days of the church had died by this time. Some had died during the persecution of Nero.

        2. It would be encouraging for Peter to assure his readers that those individuals, though dead, were alive "according to God in regard to the spirit."

    B. The translators of the New International Version obviously support this interpretation.

        1. The Greek text simply reads, *nekrois eueggelisthe*, "good news was preached to the dead."

        2. Translators added the words "those who are now [dead]" to encourage this interpretation.

II. **PETER MAY HAVE BEEN REFERRING TO A SPECIAL APPEARANCE OF CHRIST IN THE SPIRIT WORLD AFTER HIS CRUCIFIXION.**

    A. This viewpoint would correlate to the extreme literal interpretation of 1 Peter 3:18-20.

        1. These verses would be interpreted as Jesus' spirit descending into the abode of the dead while his body was in the tomb.

        2. At that time he preached the gospel message to those who had died.

B. This view does not have much scriptural support.
1. Such a view seems to offer a second chance for salvation.
2. Other than one particular interpretation of 1 Peter 3:18-20, Scripture denies the possibility of a second chance for salvation. (See Matthew 25:41, 46; Jeremiah 13:23; John 5:18, 29; Hebrews 9:27; and Revelation 22:10-12.)

III. PETER MAY HAVE BEEN REFERRING TO THOSE WHO ARE SPIRITUALLY DEAD WHILE LIVING IN THIS WORLD.

A. Other places in Scripture clearly refer to those who are spiritually dead in sin (John 5:24, 25; Ephesians 2:1, 5).

B. Many church leaders including Erasmus (Catholic) and Luther (Protestant) have supported this interpretation.

C. The language and context seem to counter this interpretation, however. Preaching to those spiritually dead still continues, but the language of the text is "was preached," referring to a completed, non-continuing action.

IV. PETER MAY HAVE BEEN REFERRING TO A PROCLAMATION IN THE SPIRIT WORLD THAT THE WORK OF SALVATION HAD BEEN COMPLETED.

A. "Preached even to the dead" means that the facts of the prophesied plan of salvation were announced to the righteous dead of all previous generations as having been completed.

B. If 3:19 involves the pronouncement of judgment upon fallen angels and the consequence of their sin upon man, would it not be proper to announce glad tidings of salvation to those who like Abraham (Romans 4:3, 17-22) were justified by faith?

Christian Conduct and Service

1 Peter 4:7-11

Peter knew that righteousness was more than a lofty ideal. Professing to love righteousness without practicing it amounts to hypocrisy. Peter describes two practices of the Christian life dedicated to righteousness.

I. LIVE AS IF THIS WERE YOUR LAST DAY OF LIFE (v. 7).

A. "The end of all things is near."
   1. Death and judgment are inevitable.
   2. The promised return of our Lord is certain. Peter started this letter speaking of the day "when Jesus Christ is revealed" (1:7), an act of God's power "ready to be revealed in the last time" (1:5).

B. "Be clear minded and self-controlled."
   1. Jesus instructed his disciples to "watch and pray" on the night of his arrest (Matthew 26:41).
   2. Jesus warned that this mental alertness needs to be an attribute of those waiting for his return (Mark 13:33-37).

II. SERVE AS THOUGH YOU WERE THE LEAST IMPORTANT PERSON ON EARTH (vv. 8-11).

A. Selfless love brings unity to the body of Christ and "covers over a multitude of sins."
   1. Setting love above all echoes the advice of Paul to the divided church in Corinth (1 Corinthians 13:13).
   2. Love and forgiveness shown to others will enable us to accept love and forgiveness from God (Matthew 5:7; 6:12).
   3. Acts of love inspire love in response. Because God loved us, we respond with love for others (1 John 4:9-11).

B. Hospitality demonstrates love and builds community.
   1. Being hospitable builds relationships with each other and with God (Hebrews 13:1, 2).
   2. Hospitality must be modeled by church leaders (1 Timothy 3:2).
   3. Hospitality, like other forms of giving, is to be practiced with a cheerful spirit (1 Peter 4:9; 2 Corinthians 9:7).

4. This type of hospitality resulted in the early church being "one in heart and mind" (Acts 4:32-34).

C. Christian service demonstrates and draws attention to God's attributes.
  1. Our abilities by which we serve are not earned or created by us. They are concrete gifts bestowed by a gracious creator, each one demonstrating God's nature in one form or another.
  2. By using these gifts for others, we are displaying God's attributes in a way that will be clearly seen by the recipient of our service.

ILLUSTRATIONS

Watch and pray. In the days of westward expansion, circuit-riding preacher, "Raccoon" John Smith, pulled alongside a parson from another church. Soon, a cold, driving rain forced the rival men of God to take cover in an inn. There they each ordered a drink to fend off the cold. Smith took his libation and immediately consumed it.

His feisty colleague coldly remarked, "You Campbellites claim to speak where the Scriptures speak. But the Bible instructs us to give thanks for everything!"

He piously closed his eyes, bowed his head, and gave thanks for his beverage. During his prayer Smith took the preacher's glass and drank all its contents. When his antagonist opened his eyes to find his glass empty, he was greeted with Smith's wry observation: "I believe the Bible also tells us to *watch* and pray".

The cost of hospitality. In the early days of the church, identifying oneself as a Christian, even to offer assistance to a stranger, presented a danger. Therefore, Christians often used the symbol of a fish to identify one another. The Greek word for "fish" (*ichthus*), became an acrostic that survives to this day. The letters of the word represent the first letters of the words in this phrase: "Jesus Christ, God's Son (and) Savior."

Humble service. At times, professional athletes do not perform with humility. It is not unusual for a football player, after running for a touchdown, to focus every eye upon himself with an "end zone dance." There was a time when such actions were not tolerated. Paul Brown, coach of the Cleveland Browns and later of the Cincinnati Bengals, once chided his players, "If you get into the end zone, act like you have been there before."

Judgment at God's House

1 Peter 4:17-19

At one time, Peter probably believed that the life of a believer should be filled with blessing and free of pain. For example, when coming upon a blind man during Jesus' ministry, the apostles assumed that his suffering was the direct result of his sin or the sin of his family (John 9:2).

This belief, widespread yet today, certainly would have caused confusion and doubt to Christians facing the persecution of Nero. Why should the faithful have to suffer?

Peter told his audience, "Do not be surprised at the painful trial you are suffering, as though something strange [foreign] were happening to you" (v. 12). He continued by explaining that "it is time for judgment to begin with the family of God" (v. 17). Peter notes two purposes for a suffering church.

I. PERSECUTION PURIFIES THE CHURCH.

A. There are weeds in God's kingdom (Matthew 13:24-30, 36-43).

1. True disciples are planted by Jesus in the field of the world (vv. 37, 38).
2. False disciples are planted in the same field by the Enemy (vv. 38, 39).
3. Angels will be the agents of judgment. They alone have been authorized to separate the "weeds" from the "wheat" at the end of the age (vv. 39-42).
4. Distinguishing true disciples from false should not be done by human wisdom alone. In performing this job delegated to angels, one could destroy the true "wheat" in the process (v. 29).

B. Persecution of the church is the beginning of this final judgment (1 Peter 4:17, 18).

1. It is not easy to live the Christian life. It demands great discipline and strain of spiritual muscle.
2. There are pretenders in the kingdom. They "choose to be Christian" for reputation, business, or political advantage.
3. In times of persecution, those whose righteousness is pretense will not remain.

II. PERSECUTION FOSTERS DEPENDENCE UPON GOD ALONE FOR SALVATION (v. 19).

A. The victory is assured because of faith.

1. "Everyone who believes that Jesus is the Christ is born of God" (1 John 5:1).
2. "This is the victory that has overcome the world, even our faith" (1 John 5:4).
3. "Therefore, since we have been justified through faith, we have peace with God" (Romans 5:1). Faith is the only door through which man may enter the throne room of grace.

B. Forgiveness is granted by God's grace.
1. Any claim that one has attained a sinless life is a lie (John 1:8).
2. The doctrine of "the absolute holiness of the saint" attained through a "second work of grace" has no solid biblical support.
3. The apostle John included himself as a sinner when he wrote, "If we confess our sins, he is faithful and just and will forgive us our sins" (1 John 1:9).
4. Paul did not hesitate to confess personal pain. "What I want to do I do not do, but what I hate I do" (Romans 7:15).
5. Neither apostle committed anything like "a sin that leads to death" which would plague him with continuous guilt and ultimate condemnation (1 John 5:16, 17). Only a complete apostasy and abandonment of the Christian system and its Savior can lead to eternal condemnation (Hebrews 6:4-6).

CONCLUSION

While persecution is painful, it is also purposeful. God in his sovereignty uses persecution to separate false disciples from the fold. Furthermore, Christians undergoing trial recognize their own inability to effect their own salvation. As judgment begins in God's household, believers are purified and strengthened.

The Shepherd and the Flock

1 Peter 5:1-11

In his first epistle, Peter gave instruction to "God's elect" urging consistent Christian living in the face of great opposition and suffering. He was martyred not much later, faithfully practicing his own advice. Leadership example is important.

As he was ready to close this letter, Peter described what it meant to lead and to follow in the church of God.

I. **CHURCH LEADERS MUST TEND THE FLOCK OF GOD (vv. 1-4).**
   A. Peter addresses elders and identifies himself as a "fellow elder."
      1. The Greek word *presbuteros*, translated "elder," is similar to the word *presbutes*, simply meaning "old man" (Philemon 9).
      2. An elder is an "older one" with the wisdom of experience. Maturity is an absolute essential to the office.
   B. Church leaders are to be shepherds or caretakers.
      1. To be caring, an elder must possess the love and compassion of Christ. The "Chief Shepherd" should be his example and guide.
      2. "The law was given through Moses; grace and truth came through Jesus Christ" (John 1:17). The elder must not be a legalistic "grace strangler" but a "grace giver."
   C. These leaders serve as overseers, taking responsibility for the direction and operation for that local part of God's family of which they are members.
      1. The Greek word translated "overseer" is *episkopos*. A compound of *epi*, meaning "over," and *skopeo*, meaning "to look" (note the similarity to the English word, "scope"), it means literally "one who looks over."
      2. Far too many church leaders are satisfied just to overlook.
      3. Elders should be "able to teach" (1 Timothy 3:2). How does one give leadership instruction who cannot teach?
   D. Church leaders should be "eager to serve."
      1. An elder is not under obligation from without but is compelled inwardly by great desire (1 Timothy 3:1).
      2. Willingness and desire take precedence over all other motives.

II. THE FLOCK IS RESPONSIBLE TO RESPOND TO GODLY LEADERSHIP (vv. 5-11).

A. Followers need to "be submissive," placing themselves under the authority of godly leaders.

1. Of what value is a quality shepherd if the flock will not follow?
2. Basic to the flock is the essential Christian virtue of humility. By following godly leaders we humble ourselves before God, trusting him to uplift us.

B. Followers must release their anxieties into God's care.

1. This is almost the tender concept of an infant in complete repose upon a mother's breast.
2. This is a John leaning back on the breast of his Master at the last supper (John 13:23).
3. In some ways this language seems strange coming from the pen of the impulsive Peter. How he mellowed!

C. Followers must recognize the reality of spiritual warfare.

1. We must be self-controlled and alert, since the devil is always poised to attack.
2. The most effective means of resisting Satan is "standing firm in the faith."
3. We can be comforted knowing that however Satan attacks, we are not alone. The universal flock struggles and suffers in the same way.

ILLUSTRATIONS

Respect for elders. As a result of my travels, I can give testimony to the fact that those of age are honored in Eastern cultures. At every social function and most noticeably at airports by customs officials, my wife and I were treated far differently from more youthful travelers.

Satanic attack. As I complete this book (1-22-99), word has come from India of greatly increased persecution against Christians—rape, murder, and burning of houses and church buildings. Religious extremists are pressuring those who have accepted Christ to turn back to Hinduism. The government is not interfering and is thought by some to be promoting the anti-Christian movement. The Lalls and J. Henry sent request for our urgent prayers. I have taught these missionaries in the U.S.A. and also in India. My heart breaks for them and for those with whom they serve.

Revelation and Inspiration

2 Peter 1:12-21

Peter was a disciple of the One who claimed to embody truth (John 14:6). Peter knew from Jesus that truth was a mark of his disciples, and that truth liberated people from the bonds of this world (John 8:31, 32).

Yet he knew that simply claiming to have truth was not enough. From where does truth come? How do we know we possess truth? Peter addressed these questions in claiming that the message that he was delivering was revealed by God and inspired by the Holy Spirit.

I. **REVELATION IS THE COMMUNICATION OF GOD'S WILL TO INDIVIDUALS.**

    A. Peter wrote to enhance and expand understanding of God's plan for humankind that his readers already possessed (vv. 12-15).

        1. Peter wrote to "remind" and to "refresh" their memories. His audience had already benefited by apostolic teaching. These readers had received his first letter and had come to the faith through the missionary work of Paul. Though "established in the truth," they still could benefit from additional teaching. We must always be willing to learn.

        2. As one to whom God had revealed truth, Peter had a limited window of opportunity to share that truth. He would soon be martyred. Until that time he needed to share God's words to him so that those words would not be forgotten after he left this earth. Teachers must always be ready to teach.

    B. Peter wrote because the message he had to give was trustworthy (vv. 16-18).

        1. Claiming to have "a word from the Lord" is not sufficient. True revelation has marks of reliability. Peter's message was not based upon "cleverly invented stories." He spoke and wrote objective history of Jesus based upon three years as an eyewitness to the ministry of Jesus.

        2. Peter not only witnessed Jesus' ministry, but he also heard God's testimony claiming and honoring his Son. On the mount of transfiguration Peter, as well as James and John, heard the voice of God himself.

        3. On the descent from the mountain the disciples received revelation concerning the death and resurrection of Jesus (Mark 9:9, 10; Matthew 17:9).

C. Peter's revelation further verified previous revelation from God (v. 19).

1. Although Peter and his audience had confidence in the utterances of the Old Testament prophets, the eyewitness testimony of the fulfillment of those prophecies made their veracity more certain.

2. By more completely providing light in the darkness of this world, revelation gives us more reason to pay attention to previous revelation until all of God's words are completely fulfilled.

II. INSPIRATION IS THE SUPERVISION OF THE HOLY SPIRIT TO ASSURE REVELATION IS ACCURATELY RECORDED AND COMMUNICATED.

A. Truth comes from outside of human beings, no matter how noble or enlightened the person (vv. 20, 21a).

1. The word translated "interpretation" is *epilusis*. This compound word comes from *epi*, meaning "in" and *lusis*, meaning "that which is loosed." In other words, an interpretation is an idea which was in existence in an individual, but had to be loosened, dug out, and freed.

2. Greek philosophers taught that truth existed within people, but needed to be freed through education and enlightenment.

3. Peter's words are a straightforward attack on that philosophy. The truth revealed by the prophets were not just good ideas they were able to excavate from within themselves. True prophecy does not originate in the mind of man but in the mind of God.

4. Paul commended the Thessalonians because they accepted the gospel that he preached "not as the word of men, but as it actually is, the word of God" (1 Thessalonians 2:13).

B. Once prophets receive the truth from God they are "carried along" by the Holy Spirit to assure that the truth remains pure (v. 21).

1. Peter was with Jesus three years before the Lord was crucified. It was more than thirty years later that Peter wrote his epistles. Time dims recollection and potential human error is always present. The oversight of the Holy Spirit was absolutely essential to errorless Scripture.

2. Jesus had promised that the Holy Spirit would remind the disciples of everything that he had taught them (John 14:26). The inspiration of the Spirit kept the revelation given by Jesus accurate in the minds of Peter and the other disciples.

CONCLUSION

The testimony we have in Scripture is wholly trustworthy. It came from the heart and mind of God and its accuracy was preserved by the Holy Spirit. The revelation of truth from God and the supervision of the recording by the Holy Spirit caused those books and letters which are collected to be our Bible to be without error.

An Assessment of False Teachers

2 Peter 2:1-22

Peter closes chapter one of his second letter with statements of assurance about prophecy which has origin with God. God's Word illuminates and is protected and kept from error by the Holy Spirit.

After making these statements about truth, he opens chapter two warning about false teachers who "introduce destructive heresies." In this chapter he discusses the condemnation false teachers bring upon themselves and others.

I. **PETER GIVES THREE REASONS WHY WE KNOW THAT GOD WILL PUNISH FALSE TEACHERS.**

   A. God imprisoned rebellious angels (v. 4).

   1. The word translated "hell" in this passage is *tartarus*. This is the only time this word is used in the New Testament.
   2. The Greek word *gehenna* is the word usually translated as "hell," and has reference to the "lake of fire" and eternal punishment (Revelation 20:10, KJV).
   3. Hell is not a place where the devil and demons rule as it is popularly portrayed. Rather eternal fire is prepared for the punishment of the devil and his angels (Matthew 25:41).
   4. Hell is final, and no creature will be there until after God's final judgment. This passage indicates that these fallen angels are kept in Tartarus, not Hell, until judgment has occurred (v. 4; Jude 6).

   B. God destroyed the ancient world with a flood (v. 5).

   1. God acted because he saw "that every inclination of the thoughts of his [man's] heart was only evil all the time" (Genesis 6:5).
   2. In the midst of this judgment, God saved righteous Noah and his family.

   C. God condemned the cities Sodom and Gomorrah (vv. 6-10).

   1. Those godless cities were annihilated by fire.
   2. These cities were filled with violence and sexual sin (Genesis 19).
   3. Lot, who was distressed by the sinful condition, was delivered.
   4. Those who likewise follow the sinful lusts of the flesh and ignore God's authority cannot escape judgment (v. 10).

II. PETER LISTS FOUR SINS COMMITTED BY FALSE TEACHERS.

A. False teachers are irreverent (vv. 10-13a).
1. False teachers are bold enough to slander angels. (See also Jude 8, 9.)
2. False teachers also speak derogatorily of God. Blasphemy is language designed to cause harm. In their foolishness they strike out at God, only to "be paid back with harm for the harm they have done."

B. False teachers are immoral (vv. 13b, 14, 18).
1. What men normally reserve for action under the cover of darkness they do in broad daylight.
2. These days it is common for talk about "coming out of the closet," meaning living a sinful life openly.
3. Additionally, false teachers pray upon the most vulnerable, seducing them to join their immoral practices.

C. False teachers are materialistic (vv. 15, 16).
1. Balaam is an example of one who was willing to let wealth lead him away from the will of God (Numbers 22).
2. Even we may find examples of religious leaders who sell out to greed.

D. False teachers reject pure doctrine (vv. 17-22).
1. They practice a form of religion that is empty. While their style is appealing, they are unable to substantially renew or refresh.
2. They promise freedom while they live in bondage to their own sinful practices.
3. When we survey the history of religious heresies, it is easy to find a correlation between false doctrine and loose morality.

CONCLUSION

If the characteristics and influence of false teachers are so repulsive to man, what must they be to God? Christians must be diligent to avoid errors in doctrine and in life. God knows how to save his own.

The End of the World

2 Peter 3:1-18

Many of us recall singing along with a popular song of a number of years ago. "Sunrise, Sunset" crooned of life continuing, unchanged, in an endless cycle. Though beautiful, the message of the song itself was false. The world will not continue forever in an endless cycle of sunrises and sunsets. One day human history will come to a close.

Jesus predicted that fallen human beings will continue to live as though there will always be a tomorrow, as did people in Noah's day (Matthew 24:38). Peter warned of the nature of coming judgment and how Christians should behave in light of it.

I. **THE END OF THE WORLD WILL BE A TIME OF DESTRUCTION (vv. 1-7).**

   A. God's powerful creative word also brings judgment.

   1. The world and all that is in it were brought about by the creative word of God. The phrase, "God said," appears ten times in Genesis, chapter one.

   2. The "same word" brings judgment. Mockers forget that the story of Noah and the flood begins with those same two words—"God said." The creative word of the Lord also predicts the end of the world and judgment.

   B. The same message was declared by God's servants who have consistently taught that God will bring this world to an end.

   1. The Old Testament prophets predicted that God will come with fire and execute judgment (Isaiah 66:15, 16; Malachi 4:1; Daniel 7:9, 10).

   2. The apostles of the New Testament echo the warnings of the prophets and agree with them (2 Thessalonians 1:7; Revelation 20:14, 15).

II. **THE END OF THE WORLD WILL BE A TIME OF RESTORATION (vv. 8-10, 13).**

   A. The present cosmic system has limits. It will "disappear . . . be destroyed by fire . . . laid bare."

   1. Jesus said that while God's message through him is eternal, the present physical world is not (Matthew 24:35).

   2. Paul viewed the present creation as a woman in labor awaiting delivery (Romans 8:20-22).

   3. John knew that the process of deterioration had already begun. About 95 A.D. he wrote in the present tense, "The world and its desires pass away" (1 John 2:17).

4. The process will come to a climactic end and without any sign or warning (Matthew 24:42-44).

B. A new, eternal creation will take the place of the old, fallen one.
1. Pristine purity will be restored. After creation and before the fall, God saw that the world was "very good" (Genesis 1:31). Likewise, the new heaven and earth will be "the home of righteousness."
2. Peter's brief statement of a new Heaven and earth is greatly enlarged upon by John (Revelation 21:1-5).
3. The prophets witnessed concerning this restoration.
   a. There will be peace and harmony in a world which is full of the knowledge of God (Isaiah 11:6-9).
   b. There the redeemed will be crowned with "everlasting joy," final condition of the redeemed (Isaiah 35:10).
   c. Tremendous change will occur to believers who are residents in that new realm (1 Corinthians 15:51-55).
4. Peter stated that Paul wrote "some things that are hard to understand" (v. 16). Paul also wrote some things very simply. It is clear that we are buried a natural body and raised a spiritual body (1 Corinthians 15:44).

III. THE IMPENDING END OF THE WORLD SHOULD BRING THE BELIEVER MOTIVATION (vv. 11-18).
A. These prophetic truths should prompt one to live a holy, godly life.
1. We must make every effort to greet the coming Lord as his pure, spotless bride.
2. As we await his coming we must grow in grace and in knowledge of him.

B. The loving heart of God is central to Peter's instruction.
1. God is patient.
2. God is not willing that any should perish.

ILLUSTRATION
New, spiritual bodies. I listened to college students discussing exactly when the saints of God would receive new, spiritual bodies. Will it be in the grave, just as they are resurrected, or in the air, as they are caught up to be with the Lord? The answer is, "Who cares?" All one needs to know is that he does not need to worry about an undertaker when he has an "upper-taker"!